Panda B

AT HOME IN THE BAMBOO GROVE

ILLUSTRATED BY DEBBIE PINKNEY
WRITTEN BY SARAH TOAST

NEW SEASONS
PUBLISHING

Copyright © 1995 Publications International, Ltd.
ISBN 0-7853-1218-8
Leap Frog is a trademark of Publications International, Ltd.

It is late summer in the steep and rocky mountains of China. In the mist of twilight, Mother Panda stirs.

Mother Panda leaves her den to climb farther down the side of the mountain. She follows long paths and tunnels that connect her den with the feeding places where she will eat from bamboo trees all night. 🐾🐾

Mother Panda wanders in the cool, damp mist through bamboo thickets sheltered by evergreen trees. She is always looking for good places to eat.

Mother Panda has an extra "thumb" that lets her handle the bamboo leaves, stems, and shoots with great care. Mother Panda spends most of her time eating the tough bamboo. 🐾

In the gray dawn, Mother Panda climbs back up the side of the mountain and enters her cave. There she gives birth to her tiny baby. Panda Baby is pink, with only a small amount of fur. His eyes are closed, but he has a loud squeal.

Mother Panda cradles Panda Baby against her chest with her large forepaws. 🐾🐾

Mother Panda stays in the den with Panda Baby. She nurses her baby, but for several days she does not go out to find food for herself.

In only a month, Panda Baby has the same warm fur coat as his mother. Not long after that, his eyes open. From then on, Mother Panda can take her cub out of the den.

Mother Panda carries Panda Baby everywhere for a long time. Mother Panda can carry her cub using her mouth. She gently picks him up and is very careful to make sure that little Panda Baby won't fall.

It is late in the autumn when Panda Baby learns to stand up. In early winter, Panda Baby is finally able to run and play.

Mother Panda and her Panda Baby roam the bamboo groves to find enough food for the hungry mother. While his mother eats, Panda Baby clowns and plays in the leaves. He isn't old enough to eat bamboo yet.

During the day, Mother Panda and her cub find places to rest in hollow trees, caves, and other rocky places.

Panda Baby gets bigger and stronger. He goes with his mother on longer walks up and down the side of the mountain and through the dense forest. They wade across streams and swim rivers. They climb trees.

The first snow of winter will soon fall. After a day of playing and exploring, Panda Baby rests in his den.

Panda Baby wakes up to his first snowfall. He loves the cold snowflakes! Panda Baby wakes Mother Panda and then does a handspring to show his delight.